MONICA LEE DISCOLO

I can't get rid of your wallpaper

a collection of whispers

Monica Lee Discolo

Love, light, + candle light.
Best wishes!
Monica

For my father and best friend, Danny

CONTENTS

loop

forgiving me

knots in my long hair

9930 54th

small victories

idle

bathing in dirt

making it count

3.

frustrated

when I get home

racing

you're the sassiest on Fridays

boil

unlikely

3:41 A.M.

fourteen

wildfire eyes

the youngest have all the merit

4.

wings

valentine in the sky

I wear you to work too

auntie Susan

w. w.

untitled

5.

a simple response

belong

I can't get rid of your wallpaper

at ease

I'm begging you to decorate

j. m.

you ought to be a harpist

daily

marking the marked

three's company

venom that restores all

MONICA LEE DISCOLO

ACKNOWLEDGMENTS

I would like to thank all of the strangers I have met at some point in passing that sparked ideas and inspired me to write unknowingly. I genuinely give my appreciation to my family and dear friends, as you are what keeps me afloat even when I've sunk to the bottom. Lastly, a heartfelt thank you to those whom I have loved and lost way too soon. My drive and passion would not exist without loss and restructure, so for you, I am eternally grateful.

1.

*sometimes I inject myself with
sugar to see if it'll make me happy*

pump

where is my thermometer?
I need some water
my body is dehydrated
I am pale in the face

my flesh is discolored
eyes glossy and wide
I have never felt better
so madly entangled

my blood has thinned
I drained it for you
you need it more
warm and clean

hook me up to your IV
I will always breathe life
into your lungs
until mine are airless

come get your fix
then look around
I will still be there
holding you close

feeling your glow
rubbing your temple

thicken my blood
pump me back up

my cells are healthy
pores like new
no longer on E
longing for this

when you are lonely
find me here to
give you my pulse
I am so ready

ingrained in my skin

you're keeping me awake
it is 4:29 in the morning
I want to be wrapped up in your eyes
feel your fingertips on my skin
I want to roll over in the night
to feel you breathing
your heart beat is my favorite song
I need your pulse on repeat
download it to my device
or on a tiny flash drive
but even if you don't
it is ingrained in my skin
I feel your heart thumping
it is entangled with mine
you go to sleep and it slips away
to come lay with me
whispers in my ear all night
the words too nervous to say
dreaming of your fingers in my strands
arm resting upon my waist
holding me so tightly yet loose
you weave me in your veins
my heart melts into a puddle
that spills across the floor
gather me up into a mason jar
you know I like those best

keep me with you through it all
sip from me when you are feeling lonely
and when you are nervous or enamored
anytime you feel anything
I am yours if you'll have me
flying through the air
laying with you always
kissing your sleeping eyes
I am with you tonight
in dreams and in thought
you are my beating heart

January the 24th

just another calendar date
to the average shmuck

just another day to my withered father
who loves the word shmuck

just another day to the cashier at the store
where I waste my money
buying toxins to create a mask

just another day to the realtor
closing on a deal

just another day in year '89
when a new son was welcomed

just another day to the sun
who went to sleep dreaming of the moon

just another day to the homeless man
trying to get the remote in the day room

just another day to the judge
sentencing someone to a new life

just another day to be alive

functioning and existing idly

the ground shook with the universe speaking
fate made a promise

to be met five years forward
when the clouds opened their eyes

just another day to you
but the most critical to me

after waiting for several lifetimes
my soulmate was finally born

lifeline

my universe is harsh and freezing
you are my blanket
always I am hurting
but I ache for you

my desired pain is that of
you yanking my heart strings
playing them like a harp
a melody unique to you and I

I feel love from my throbbing heart
down through to my palms
each nerve weaving about
telling the store of us

feeling you swimming in my veins
I hope you stay there

buried in the same coffin

first day, you open your eyes
you blink, you're 19
pick up a pen, and find the one
spend every millisecond
making them smile
pleasing their every atom
kissing each individual cell
in this life and in the next
until death do us part
but even after that
my bones will crisp post mortem
from holding your hands too tight
ready I will be for part two
of our second life
from this life to the next
I will always enter with you
buried in the same coffin
our souls will spin and dance
forever moving, mixing
like the first day we met
I will always find you
but for today, for tomorrow
I will enjoy you in this form

tandem

you are the love of my life
I am sure of it, it's true
but I don't even know your last name
and you don't know mine, do you?

our love trumps time and space
we are to be together, this I'm sure
but I don't even know your birthday
or what makes you insecure

I can picture us at the altar
taking big steps fairly soon
but I don't know if you like to sunbathe
or prefer admiring the moon

I'm making us plans for the future
just assuming you are too
but I don't even know where you reside
or when I could come see you

none of these details matter
it's undeniable that we are in sync
our souls are in tandem
I would give you my heart, I think

4:02 A.M.

why do these thoughts come out to play
when the neighborhood cats do
thoughts dance in my head all day
but I cannot grasp them
they only slow down when the night does
just close enough for me to reach
but not close enough to secure a grip
my mind knows of the love I feel
but this heart is so stubborn
my lips won't release how I feel
like my love is locked in a coffin
I just want to send you my feels
you call me and I choke up
why can't I say it
I am so in love with you
but these words aren't enough for me
I'll search the dictionary until my fingers wrinkle
to find the words that will match
and maybe by your 60th birthday
I'll find some words that are worthy
of your everlasting love

glass that won't cut my hands

seeing you shattered the windows
of our little glass hut
we gazed and time stopped
your half crumbled
mine to melt apart
we began collecting the glass pieces
but I grabbed some of yours
similar, I mistake them for my own
I take your pieces along with me
but I'll leave you some behind
hold onto them with white knuckles
while I try to put them back together
using my heart strings as glue
but this puzzle will not be finished
until I am alone with you
you are my one true half
you are my left fuzzy slipper
the sand in my hour glass
the hair pins I can never find
morning frost on my windshield
the essence of my mind

flesh

I am merely flesh
one human being
flawed and damaged

all I can give another
is my attitude
along with a side of
corny jokes and nervous laughs

add another order of
sensitivity and indecisiveness
add a long list of imperfections
no one wants to receive

a short list of undesirable qualities
I can hand them over to you

every night and throughout each day
I can kiss your wounds
show you it is not always so bad

I can give you small things
tokens of affection
and genuine stares

every atom of my soul

will read your name
and I will love you

rock climbing minus the rocks

breathe in
breathe it out
breathe again
recharge your lungs
exhale all that
you're fixating on
those harbors
are not yours

you can carry but one oxygen tank

mediocre

I wake up
curse the day
put on my collared shirt
feed the pets
turn the house alarm on
defrost the windshield
now I'm on my way
look at my screen
until my head aches
another wasted day
mediocre
human condition
work and work with no play
this life is dull
but this love is not
we'll be together someday
you are my substance
let me abuse you
you taste better anyway
than the most expensive alcohol
asleep with my glasses on
wake up again
same routine
maybe tomorrow you'll call

2.

*sometimes I smell the dirty roses
and take it all in*

I *looked around*

I looked around, dodging polite smiles
where is their compassion?
how can they stare, how can they whisper
without knowing my story?

grey smirks, sharp opinions
I'm on a social operating table
under the knife, painful remarks
they sit there and mock my behavior

I looked around, and what I found
it was I looking in the mirror
I am judging those who judge me
I am the only one here who is harsh

loop

internal spotted race
life is humming deafly
few answer the call
the yellow dust phone

work and no play
dull boy syndrome
each day mimics
one of last dream

rhythm with no pulse
dance without beat
moving about frazzled
a clock with no pause

take out for lunch
but indefinitely out
ends meet stood us up
who feeds the feeding hand?

eat the dinner cooked
under rest, over slept
the moon's ex-lover
bargain for some rest

forgiving me

when I think of forgiving myself
I rack my brain of tragic memories
trying to make sense of it all
but really I crave forgiveness
for everyday inconveniences
forgetting to hold the door for the next
pardoning myself for chewing loudly
burning my breakfast toast
locking myself out of the house
spilling something on my shirt
not remembering to take out the trash
minor infractions but major to me
daily faults I dwell over
no one is tougher on me than I
though a tragic past belongs
I need to conquer the trivial things
to begin the healing process
of feeling me forgiving me

knots in my long hair

depression is
avoiding doctor appointments
not wearing my seat belt
crying in the shower
leaving the doors unlocked on purpose

depression is
forgetting my own birthday
wearing the same shirt for three days
knots in my long hair
blood gums when I finally brush

depression is
moldy bread on the counter
smiling in the public eye
eating my salty tear drops
only alcohol in the refrigerator

depression is
buying things to make myself smile
knick-knacks all over the house
not clipping my toe nails
forgetting to feed the dog

depression is
forgetting to bring my cell phone

being late to each obligation
not taking a lunch break
failing on purpose

depression is
crumpled up poetry attempts
laughter with distant family
a forever staying roommate
somehow my only best friend

9930 54th

woodwork speaks louder than me
releasing memories while containing
layers of old paint, one of new
modernized fixtures, half antique

front lawn thriving, evidence of life
internal damage scurried about
unfinished bathroom but thick toilet paper
new beach towels mixed with the old

stolen street signs line the garage
still, untouched lamps slumber inside
aged mirror, no reflection looking back
leather couch so new, no feet allowed

eerie silence encompasses tired street
house alarm breaks lack of noise
laying here in the dark and inaudible
mind more colorful than the bed sheets

small victories

I blinked my eyes twice
miss January appeared
gazing into the mirror
I look down myself
count up my blessings
trace my shortcomings
what will I change?
love and respect my temple
aid with compassion
keep up with my vegetables
take my pills on time
drink green tea before bed
a bubble bath each month
extend a hand to others
when mine is not cut off
live this year with passion
small victories do add up
fundamentals of trying
miss January will greet me tender
next time she comes around

idle

my mind is outside
I'm out there with it
my physical is in this room
weighing on my desk and chair
I am playing in the trees then
looking at the birds
from out my bedroom window
I'm napping in my room
my dreams still uncontrolled
and just what I need
it's chilly outside today
even when it's warm
this body is in a classroom
but I am somewhere far away
I'm in the solar system
floating about
while lying in the grass
having so much fun relaxing
time is flying by
oh, it's that awful time again
my body and I are meeting
now we're both in class

bathing in dirt

looking out over
can't begin describing
the scenes I have seen

film keeps going
even when I push
the double line button

trauma lives where it picks
pigment doesn't wear a
welcome home sign

it lives in me, recognizing you
this isn't me, I didn't do this
I just read pre-written stories

but them, they know it
they deserve the extra look
their stand-offs, their simple joy

they are the stories
they walk with dull purpose
but it's there, grabbing at my

throat, telling me to listen
read the thought, eat the sandwich

keep it moving in the morning

each a test to be kind to anger
scabbing feet, jittery teeth
but cleaner than us all

making it count

staggered through the waiting room
one foot in front of the other
hopped in my truck
immediately called my mother

she told me to sit and think
about the one year I was granted
and to think about this fate
as a chance to be replanted

so I started to rank
the desires I buried deep
confused whether to smile
or to silently weep

then I packed my bags
with the intent to travel
threw my truck in reverse
cut my wheels in the gravel

I craved the open sky
camping in the rocky tips
skin embracing the mist
moon kissing my lips

next, a tour to London

as an avid Winehouse fan
hung from the Eiffel Tower
well, at least that was the plan

next, I was on a farm
family owned, lots of space
picked some corn, walked the field
rubbed celosias on my face

drove to Canada, on a whim
more enjoyable than a plane
became a citizen, dabbled in French
finally got to change my name

traveled far to Finland
enrolled to start my PhD
found a charismatic Finnish tutor
I can't believe their college is free

came back to Boston to see family
I can't believe it's been half the year
saw old friends, played some Jenga
suddenly it all became clear

what I once craved, what I desired
I really didn't need at all
contacted all my friends and family
at least those who answered my call

gathered them all, in one space
my childhood home on Appleton street
played board games, indulged in laughter

together in the place we used to meet

tangled in the crowd, his eyes like a hook
my childhood crush from around the way
I stroked his chin, told him I missed his scent
and counted down until our wedding day

took his hand and his heart
walked them down the aisle too
date night on Tuesdays, football on Sunday
and plenty of "I love you"

returned to Florida, bought a home
began feeling nauseous, suddenly ill
realized now, the consequences of how
I forgot to take my prevention pill

blessed with another life and legacy
a child as regal as my story
ultrasound, baby big and round
hoped for a boy, name him Kory

one month too short for my last term
unsure our baby will make it doubts
flooded reality, motherhood appeared
then a solution I figured out

went back to the same visiting room
where I heard the daunting news
infection cleared, I am well
karma decided I paid my dues

my one year mark staring me down
making me uneasy, surely unsure
wondering if my party of two will make it
my intentions and instincts pure

the one year point passed by
still breathing strong and thriving
I have smashed my one year hour glass
I am doing more than just surviving

labor approached and delivered
a petite little girl to my surprise
our tiny princess, little miss Kory
with big blue ocean eyes

happy at home, my little family and I
not realizing I needed this all along
hearing my spouse preparing dinner
while I sing our child a lullaby song

this year I lived free from reservations
and true blessing came to me so vast
if I am lucky enough to see another year
again, I will make every minute last

3.

*sometimes I'm a swamp demon
disguised as a woman*

frustrated

blood boiling
fingers take stance
my mind circles
pulse does a dance

how could you say that
what do you mean
I always thought
you'd be on my team

but people let you down
drive you up a wall
my mood can be switched
by one phone call

phone rings and rings
and it irritates me
you ask the same question
not two times, but three

then you catch an attitude
hurt my feelings too
I'm done being frustrated
and frustrating you

when I get home

this feels like the last straw
the last chance I can take

but it's a good one

I'm not afraid of you or this
the problem doesn't lie in you

the perpetrator is me

you look into my eyes
genuine and kind hearted

how do I keep you

miles separate us momentarily
but we could overpower anything

you get me through each day

thinking of you always
dreaming of you indefinitely

I love waking up in our truth

I'm forced to crack a smile

across my canvas of life

I'm anxious to paint you on it

this will be out work of art
butterflies can live forever

I'll see you when I get home

racing

talking myself off the ledge
the brink of my heart
fuel inside me it burns
with the flames of could-haves
please help me out of the fire
but I don't want you to
I want to disintegrate to ashes
maybe then you'd sweep me up
put my remains in a jar
place me on your deception shelf
maybe I like the pain
sometimes I don't even think
I type useless words and click send
then take them all back in my head
you make a mess of me
I want you but I don't
I shake when you're near me
what if you held me?
my, what if I could hold you?
I'd be gasping for breath
days, months, years keep passing
I taste you like blood in my mouth
one day I will catch you
if you slow down and let me
come cross the finish line with me
so we can finally begin

you're the sassiest on Fridays

beauty, beauty, beauty
you're chaotic
quite the mix

¾ beauty
¼ chaotic
something missing

equate us
together
beauty, beauty, beauty, chaotic
add me
mess

beauty, beauty, beauty, chaotic, mess
written on our tomb stone

our story, nonetheless

boil

you make me feel
like I'm in a boiling pot
I cannot escape you
hovering over me
slowly burning to death
you bring my blood to a boil
set fire to my attitude
hurting me like no one does
sometimes you make me steamy
I want whatever you are cooking
but mostly I am suffocating
so deeply embedded in your sauce pan
my heart jumps more than the water does
when my asparagus is boiling
there is too much water in my pot
I am drowning slowly
but the chef won't shut off the burner
you like watching the bubbles
it intrigues you to blister me
you think it is ripening me
making me more enjoyable
but you're pushing my buttons
stirring me with a spoon
you force me into another form
until you can enjoy who I am
molding me into your meal

you eat my independence
swallow my self-esteem
hopefully I will be stable
when I realize you're not a chef
then the water stops boiling
and the kitchen is finally closed

unlikely

pulse in my hands
I have you but you're not mine
you're hers
you'll always be hers
my taking this much longer
is highly unlikely
she is in control of you
meaning she is in control of me
too many ties
surplus of them that
I cannot weave
there's not enough
string in the world
for me to combine
to create what is still ongoing
some walls can't be broken
I think ours are building
then she kicks them down
a toddler ruining our sand castle
some cement never dries
your heart is in a small bottle
carried around in her purse
notify me when it's returned
assuming I will be around
but that's also unlikely

3:41 A.M.

its 3:41
my neck hairs stand up
my muscles quiver
you're all around
suffocating me
grasping my eyelashes
your name is on my tongue
I just want to yell it
but whisper it softly
so my pillows can hear
it can settle in my blankets
and hold me tonight
because you can't

its 4:41
my eyes are red
my muscles are achy
you're dancing in my head
I wish I could tell you
call you or something
and profess my love
like they do in the movies
give you your part
what would I even write?
I want to tug your hair
feel your hands on my veins

drown in your voice

its 5:41
my lungs are lonely
sing your melody into my chest
wrap me in your impulses
sink energy into my bed frame
leave your dirty plates in my sink
I want to try this new game
tuck you in at night
hold you when you drink too much
knit you some warmer socks
keep track of your medicines
love you until it's over
and happily even after

fourteen

fourteen times I was minding my business
fourteen times you started a fight
fourteen times my eyes were blackened
fourteen times you had to be right

fourteen times I tried to let you go
fourteen times my mother shook her head
fourteen times the neighbors started whispering
fourteen times you'd force me to bed

fourteen times I fell asleep hungry
fourteen times you went through my phone
fourteen times there was a hole in the wall
fourteen times our house was not a home

fourteen times I pretended to be sleeping
fourteen times my coworkers tried to aid
fourteen times you said I couldn't do better
fourteen times you took my money when I got paid

fourteen times you said it was an accident
fourteen times I packed to leave town
fourteen times you hid my keys from me
fourteen times the stairs you pushed me down

fourteen times I read your obituary

fourteen times it mentioned your name
fourteen times won't become fifteen
fourteen times ensued but I bear no shame

wildfire eyes

no words describe my anticipation
your eyes embrace me

it is a strange fate to bear
but still I'm here waiting with anticipation
your eyes embrace me

your lock me in when you look my way
each time being different
but the same somehow
your eyes embrace me

you ask about my day
it usually is ghastly
I can't help but smile
and say it's okay
your eyes embrace me

exchanging looks one on one
close enough to hear your heart beating
but far enough not to exchange a hello
no simple indication of unity
my heart in gallows for missing you
but still I come in to see you every day
your eyes embrace me

the youngest have all the merit

how old are you?
as if that'll answer the
question that you really
want to know, as if
that will break the sneer
of what you're really asking

yes Cheryl, I am physically young
do you really want to know
how I feel? do you want
to hear the beating, and off-beat
of my mousey heart? will it
make you walk away proud

is it that intriguing to hear an
answer that you selected
before I unclenched my
pressed lips? how does this
taste? assault with later rips
and stabs, and injection shots

loud noise, calm distance
then the blow of the handle?
warm dishwashers, black iron
cups of noodles never looked
so good, rowdy children and

silent nights with one eye shut

my peroxide prerogative
has made 24 just that much
more clean, please give me
some cereal so I can learn not
to hate myself, I must have
forgot my smile in that room

my time isn't shaped by
lunch time chatting, not once
did I miss lunch, but that
doesn't mean I had money
it was shameful, please spare me
I didn't learn it in class

24 years old, but 24 times
I did it by myself, no help
no reason, I picked my own days
what you see, what I am
I take full credit for, my credit score
has seen better days, but

I'm building on cracked
foundations, thank God
I love band-aids with patterns
keep on keeping on, or some
bullshit I tell myself to keep
walking, outside to the next

day of people like you, asking
what my age is, as if you have

an indication that my daddy
must have made me smart
he sure did, he made me, and
I made myself intelligent

I buy my own toilet paper, to
wipe my own ass, but yes, Cheryl
my parents must have at least
picked out the brand, so thank you
for asking, and no I didn't get
my experience from coursework alone

in a college that I'm still paying
for, I've struggled with real people
and pulled those people out on
my own back, even when it was
broken, so I'm glad your niece
also paints like me, really I am

I don't harbor discontent for
any person doing better, I pray for
no child to ever fall down, or pull
their own teeth out of their mouth
but to each their own, my children
will never be alone, whether I'm

on the earth or not, so thank you
again for stopping by, at the end of
the day, I always say, pale people
have pale opinions, if you feel better
assigning me to a picket fence
please close my office door, thanks

MONICA LEE DISCOLO

4.

sometimes I wish I could overdose
from mourning and see you

wings

when the shadows shine in my corner
my thoughts point down
diversions fade and I wonder
what would life look like
if you were in this form
warm, heart thumping
how would I dress?
what would I say to you?
what shampoo would I be using?
would I be on the floor at 4 A.M. aching?
what would your favorite song be?
would you take the trash out?
little broken crackers
on the counter
un-mopped floor
dirty shower drain
sometimes I can't get up
sometimes I can't stop pacing
I loved you so much
that I'm having trouble loving myself
I need help with more than
everyday tasks
I need sunlight
I need an extra breath
breathe into me
push the air back into my lungs

that I inhaled when you were here
each day I'm battling the sting within
deep down in my bones I cry for you
but I am a fighter
I will get through this
invincible with you on my team
can I borrow your wings tonight?

valentine in the sky

conversation hearts, dark chocolate
flower petals line the floor
tangible signs of affection
but what I crave is unattainable

I'm writing this valentine
but I'm not sure how it is to be sent
what do I say, how do I seal it?
you know the words before they meet my pen

you weave my soul, you live in my brain
no other valentine will do
you will always be my sweetheart
I will picnic at your grave with you

and yet others may think I'm lonely
seemingly spending the day alone
I am filled with love, wrapped with care
I spray myself with your cologne

I miss you living on earth
but we are not that far apart
happy valentine's day my love
you're still the keeper of my heart

I wear you to work too

sometimes when
I sit in my car
driving back from
work, another sorry
client spit in my face
or cursed at the wind
blowing by them, you
will still table me

images flash, so I
welcome a chill, and
you are all I can
make out, nothing
in this state is
concrete, and I feel
your warm, tender
yet crisp, breath

I keep driving, unsure
how I can operate a
vehicle, when I can't
even handle your
hip bones, in
the shadow of the
sheets, your hair
in my face, somehow

glancing down, hair
strands on my pants
and I pick them
off, but they just
come back, years later
my skin cells die
but the ones wearing
your touch, remain

auntie Susan

strong calves, gabby tongue
I wanted to be just like you
thin, but thick in laughter
cancer still forcefully knocked

frail, hospice queen
headscarf coming off
tears and lungs I swallow
it has reached your brain

feeding you applesauce
smirking in my direction
gravel eyes wide you said
"they waste MORE plastic!"

just like that, made me laugh
slipping to your next life
no healing stones nor bedpan stains
could kill that wit of yours

w. w.

as the clock ticks toward twelve
I feel you more than ever
snowflakes kiss my nose
but time bites my heart
couples fill my space
in which confetti lingers
I sense reflection approaching
as you're heavy on my mind
where I will be at midnight
is just beyond this block
my toes seem to be frozen
along with my guarded heart
I finally reach your tombstone
it's covered now in frost
you were taken in the spring
it still hurts in the winter
but genuine love cannot be lost
so it's a happy new year

untitled

so it goes
you're dead
and I'm here
but I feel you
like mist in the morning
making me uncomfortable
but secure
you lost your breath
but so did I
you must have took it with you
the bullet that hit
struck me too
your soft skin
now a cold rock
your head used to lie
in the bed where I sleep
night after night
I crave your warm laughs
what has happened?
you were everything
now nothing
you're buried deep
but both our bones decompose
mine shiver with depression
yours connect with the earth
you're in the ground and sky

at the same time
but so am I
some days I'm high up
many I'm down
I wish we could go back
in the middle of the two
where I could hold your hand

5.

sometimes my veins get tangled and
I can't see

a simple response

"would you like to dance?"
those simple five words
give my heart a murmur
that I swear I was born with
his dimples cut the room
separate it into portions
the women to the right
longing for a connection
wishing for that velvet touch
all dolled up, hair coiled
sitting in ballroom chairs
compact mirrors, some engraved
the sticky dance floor waving
each floor fiber telling the story
of lovers and strangers entangled
home base of one night affairs
and 65 year marriages
swaying with him in my mind
twirling, breathing heavily
my feet going numb
moving like seaweed in the ocean
spaghetti coming to a boil
two apples dangling in a tree
his palm raises my arm hair
long hair makes me feel pretty
my dress matches his cuff links

coordination not planned
synchronized nervousness
we hasten across the floor
moonlight gazes, friends take notice
powder room conversations arise
intertwined energies wrap like blankets
I taste the whisky on his lips
slow guiding, timid smiles
forgetting the evening's newlyweds
could we be next?
my fingertips magnetic to the bouquet
his eyes fixed upon mine
hanging for a response
society caused the impulse to say
"I'm sorry, I don't dance"

belong

deep down
blue shock
warm skin
authentic

smile aches
heart raw
nervous laughter
harmony

natural light
love's remedy
arteries tangle
passion

sincere glances
chaotic silence
moon drawn
linger

soul match
fingertip bingo
beyond words
energy

mandala bliss

angled sleep
soft intuition
everlast

I can't get rid of your wallpaper

awake and look over
drooling and breathing sharp
you were slumber dreaming
not knowing you were the dream

humming lovebird ticking now
fire alarm in our funhouse
lethal means leap across
you now belong to earth

years pass truly foggy
wearing faulty eye prescriptions
living, repeating, pause
my home leaves home for now

courting attempts flood
none fill your dark void
one sparks another spark
believe the unbelievable

push passion into small space
drink their beloved potion
cram nerves in a vase
never that great at gifting

to move my home slowly

from your eyes to the next
lover brings bright wallpaper
dwelling in a mixed lounge

nourish and lick the scabs
but sunrise does bring rain
insecurities begin to peel
the wallpaper back to yours

at ease

my blood boils
you cool it down
wash away the negative
keep my feet on the ground

you are my meditation
my zen and my calm
you make my nerves dance
down through my palms

you ease my mind
when you rattle my core
you're my toes in the sand
I think I need you more

be my sea of blankets
wrapping me serene
bringing peace to my mind
on you I will lean

you chill me with love
relax me, get my blood pumpin'
you're my open field
my whole heart, slow thumpin'

I'm begging you to decorate

notecards in the late night
just us, unbothered
but all eyes on me, so
I wish you'd decorate
distract my astray pupil
that's what I do best
studying me studying you
dim walls stare back
fill the walls with artwork
things we partially believe
but nothing will fill these walls
inside of my heart
for tonight, maybe next week
you're my soul decor

j. m.

ocean water eyes, an insincere smile
Haymarket was our spot
you proposed to me in parking space six
kissed you on the roof
always loved cutting hair
so you cut all of mine off
too old for me at seventeen
mom made me cut you loose

you ought to be a harpist

you ought to be a harpist
blistered fingers, patience of a rock
with soul deeper than a shoe
with the comfort of fuzzy socks

you ought to be a harpist
producing this masterpiece of time
one only you and I can hear
the song you play over in my mind

you ought to be a harpist
with the way you play my strings
using all my woven nerves
to show me all love can bring

you ought to be a harpist
with the way you pick up the beat
strumming on my butterflies
like I'm your only music sheet

daily

you're the empty pit in my stomach that rumbles unexpectedly, always hidden from my friends

you're that crispness in the air that cuts like I Can't Believe it's Not Butter, at 5 A.M. on graduation day

you're that warm summer night where we question the very heart beats & breaks that got us here

you're the plastic piece of the tag that itches my back in my office chair but at least I got style

you're the soap scum on the wall of that shower I've sat and cried in until I couldn't recognize my hands

you're the paper towel I'm using to construct these words on, half ripped, kinda stained, full of time

you're everything I wish I retrieved when I say "no, say something nice" while painting my kitchen floor

you're the shopping bags full of new things scattered about my home, you never quite fill the void

you're a Tuesday when you love me but I'm like cheap luggage tags in the airport, looking for an owner to cling to you're the greasy food I regret eating at night, and the feeling you get when there is a fry at the bottom of the bag

you're all the space left on this napkin, your passion woven in coffee stains, I can never bleach you out

you're my whole day

marking the marked

no hickeys, no
stay slowing up
need you near
but feelings down

tugging on my
midline, zap
is this rooted in
my mental or palms

fussing and touching
on and off Jazz song
with a line missing
we hear it though

three's company

your best version of self
loves me the best
I'll push that half of you
until the other gets so mad

that it decides to meet us
both for drinks, to celebrate
all you will accomplish
and you both will drink

and drink, and laugh
wondering where the other
had been, and one will look
at me and grin, and the

other will smile back, and
the three of us will sip, each
half sharing a drink
pinpointing what to fight

about, and when reality
sinks to the bottom of your
draft and it's time to go
I'll take the whole person home

venom that restores all

love is a lifestyle
it dwindles and it sweeps
it creeps and it crawls
down deep into the core
swallowing all in its path
taking life, ah, but giving it
the new and most fragile state
but most resilient of them all
it lurks in the happy child
the old and wicked alike
inescapable is it
each harbors this poison
venom that restores all
love breaks and it takes
but gives and weaves together
shattered fragments across the floor
taken apart then assembled again
love is a process that never ends
though many long for closing
never do they quit this drug
time and time again
thy chosen lifestyle, is love

ABOUT THE AUTHOR

Monica Lee Discolo is a poet whose works have appeared in *Grey Dawn* and *On Earth as it is in Poetry* both by various authors, edited by Kevin Watt. Monica's poetry is driven by emotion and infatuation with life's idiosyncrasies. Monica is a doctoral candidate for a PhD in Human and Social Services, with a graduate degree in in Criminal Justice and an undergraduate degree in Human Development. Monica is versatile and wears many hats as a social worker, dispatcher, artist, poet, animal lover, lifelong learner, and many other roles. Monica is originally from Saugus, Massachusetts and is currently enjoying life in the St. Petersburg, Florida area.

Made in the USA
Monee, IL
08 February 2020